I'M SO LUCKY
I NEVER GET CAUGHT
WRITING GRAF

Seamus O'Leary/O'Larry

IRISH GRAFFITI

Futura
Macdonald & Co
London & Sydney

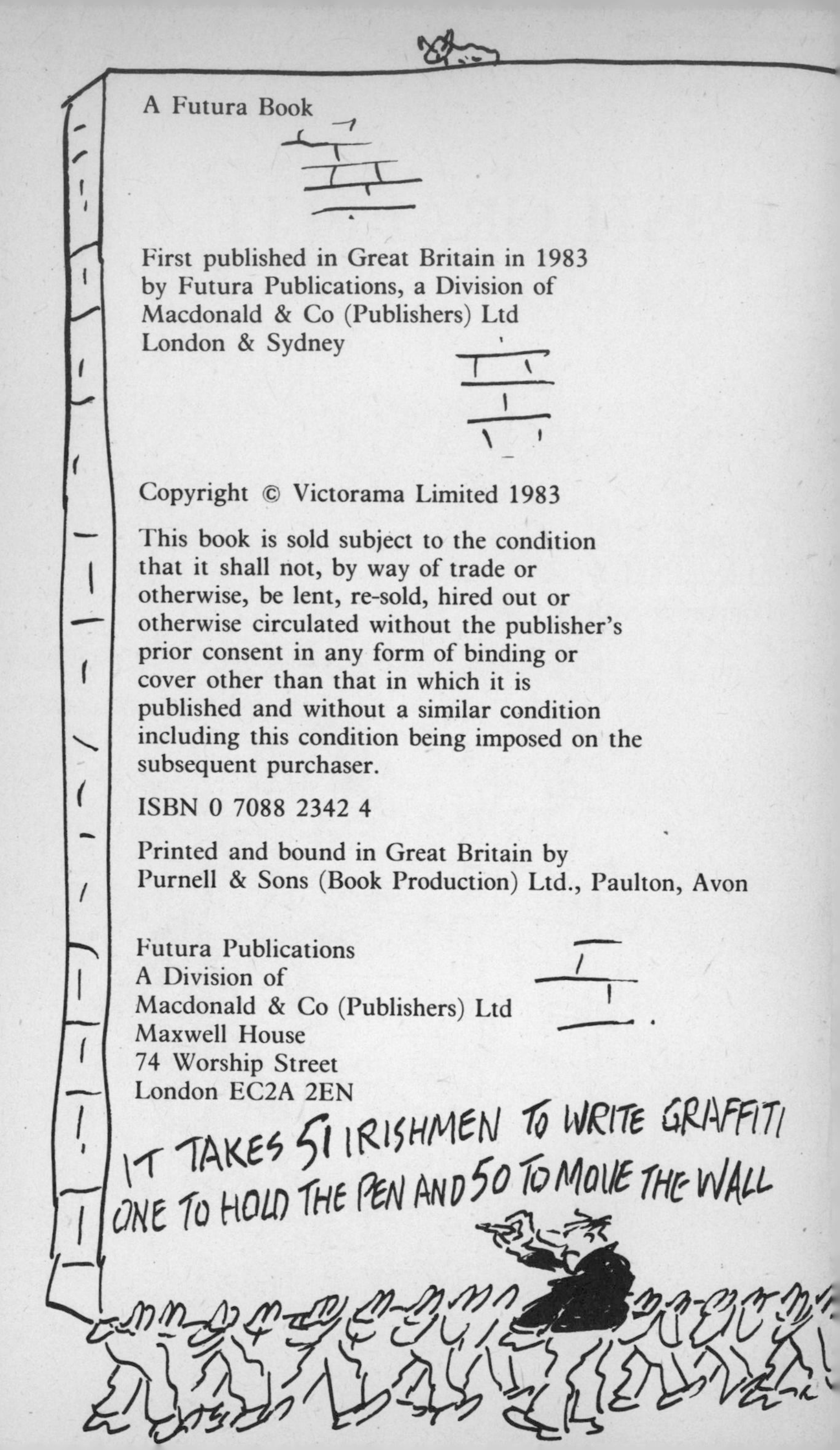

A Futura Book

First published in Great Britain in 1983
by Futura Publications, a Division of
Macdonald & Co (Publishers) Ltd
London & Sydney

ISBN 0 7088 2342 4

Printed and bound in Great Britain by
Purnell & Sons (Book Production) Ltd., Paulton, Avon

Futura Publications
A Division of
Macdonald & Co (Publishers) Ltd
Maxwell House
74 Worship Street
London EC2A 2EN

IRISH GRAFFITI

IRISH ADVICE
ONLY BUY A USED CAR WHEN IT'S NEW
GET OUT OF PAYING THE RENT
Always wear a hat - you'll know where to stop when you wash your face
HAVE YOUR EARS AMPUTATED.
CONFUSE AN IRISHMAN SAY HELLO TO HIM
Brainwash an Irishman - Use an enema
IRISH CITIZENS ADVICE BUREAU
EMMIGRATE

CLEAN THE INSIDE OF YOUR WINDOWS NOT THE OUTSIDE. YOU'LL BE ABLE TO SEE OUT, BUT THE NEIGHBOURS WON'T SEE IN.

Put a bucket of manure on the table - it keeps flies off the food.

PUT ONE IN THE KITCHEN, IT KEEPS THEM OUT OF THE DINING ROOM

IF YOU WANT TO RIDE MAKE SURE YOU'VE GOT A BIKE

Save shoe leather walk on your hands

JUMP OFF A CLIFF - YOU'LL BE DEAD FOR THE REST OF YOUR LIFE

Ring Irish Alcoholics Anonymous. If you feel like sobering up, someone comes round with a GUINNESS
CROSS AN IRISHMAN WITH A BOOMERANG AND YOU'LL GET A SMELL YOU CAN'T GET RID OF
LOOKING FOR A GAS LEAK? USE SAFETY MATCHES.
FOUND A GAS LEAK? PUT A BUCKET UNDER IT AND CALL THE GAS BOARD
MAKE MONEY GO FURTHER POST IT TO A DISTANT RELATIVE.
When arguing with an Irishman make sure he isn't doing the same

SWALLOW RAZOR BLADES THEY'LL SHARPEN YOUR APPETITE
IRELAND IS PROOF GOD HAS A SENSE OF HUMOUR
never hit an Irishman when he's down - he might get up again
POST EARLY FOR CHRISTMAS 2085
GO AND BITE A FISHERMAN HE MIGHT NOT HAVE HAD A BITE ALL DAY

IF YOU'RE THERE
BEFORE IT'S OVER
YOU'RE ON TIME

FOR THE
MILLIONTH
TIME
DON'T EXAGGERATE

NEVER HIT
A MAN
WITH GLASSES
USE
A
BRICK

FOREWARNED IS FOREARMED

I've only got three

you're lucky to have
three, I've
only got two

most people only have
TWO

GIRLS BE CONSTRUCTIVE MAKE LOVE TO A BRICKY
PROCRASTINATION IS A WASTE OF TIME
Join the Union Thats Going places the SOVIET UNION
BUILD A FALL-OUT SHELTER TODAY AND FRY UNDERGROUND
IF NOTHING ACTS FASTER THAN ANADIN TAKE NOTHING

HELP WILDLIFE
GIVE A BIRD A BATH
DON'T GET MAD
GET EVEN
ALWAYS PUT YOUR BEST FOOT FORWARD
ESPECIALLY WHEN WALKING
THROUGH A FIELD OF COWS
Never look for a husband
Look for a Single man
KEEP IRELAND TIDY
STAY IN BED

I'VE GOT A BAD STOMACH
WELL, KEEP YOUR COAT ON
AND NO ONE WILL NOTICE
Don't lose any sleep over Insomnia.
SAVE THE DINOSAUR BEFORE ITS TOO LATE
NEVER KISS AT THE GARDEN GATE LOVE IS BLIND BUT THE NEIGHBOURS AINT
NEVER TRY TO TEACH A PIG TO SING — IT WASTES YOUR TIME AND ANNOYS THE PIG
IF YOU CAN READ THIS YOU'RE UPSIDE DOWN

IRISH BRAINS
MURPHY MENDED 16 BROKEN WINDOWS IN HIS HOUSE, THEN HE DISCOVERED HIS GLASSES WERE CRACKED
I CALL my pet zebra 'SPOT'!
I have trouble catching grouse
YOU'RE NOT THROWING YOUR DOG UP HIGH ENOUGH
Who's been sleeping in my porridge? IRISH GOLDILOCKS
MY GOLDFISH IS DEAD – IT WAS ALRIGHT WHEN I PUT IT IN IT'S CAGE LAST NIGHT
A-LEVEL
O-LEVEL
MASTERMOIND
SPECIAL SUBJECT BRICK-LAYING 1950 – 1982
PINT-AD
EASY CROSSWORD
READERS DIGEST
IMPROVE YOUR WORDPOWER!
CAT
MAT
EGG

My cat Tinker
doe his business
and then
buries himself

How do chickens lay eggs
in the middle of
veal and ham pies?

IRISH MATERNITY HOSPITALS
HAVE A TEN MONTH
WAITING LIST

HOW DOES A ONE-MAN BUS
MOVE, WHEN THE DRIVER
IS UPSTAIRS
COLLECTING THE FARES?

Get rid
of worms
- bury them

DON'T SLIP ON
POLISHED FLOORS
- WEAR SPIKED
SHOES

I DROPPED MY CIGAR
OUTSIDE THE DOGS HOME.
PICKED UP 17 BEFORE
I FOUND THE RIGHT ONE.

IRISH LIMBO DANCERS
HAVE TROUBLE GETTING OVER
THE POLE

Two in one people
are schizophrenic
in Ireland

I'M GLAD I WASN'T BORN
IN FRANCE. I CANT
SPEAK A WORD OF FRENCH

I'D GIVE MY
RIGHT ARM
TO BE AMBIDEXTROUS

I USED TO DRESS OFF THE PEG
BUT NOW THE NEIGHBOURS
TAKE IN THEIR WASHING
AT NIGHT

ISNT IT CLEVER
HOW THE ALPHABET
IS IN ALPHABETICAL
ORDER

SUICIDE IS A DYING ART
SUICIDE IS A WAY OF LIFE
THE SAMARITANS
HAPPY HOUR 5-30 – 6-30
CLOSED EVEN FOR JUNKIES
MUMMY, DADDY JUST FELL OFF THE ROOF
I KNOW, I SAW HIM PASS THE WINDOW
I THOUGHT BASILDON BOND WERE CIGARETTES – IT TOOK ME 60oz OF TOBACCO TO FILL THE ENVELOPE AND A BLOW LAMP TO LIGHT IT

WHY AM I SO MUCH MORE NORMAL THAN EVERYBODY ELSE?

TRY SOME DOPE AND FIND OUT WHY

IT'S IMPOSSIBLE TO JUGGLE BRAINS.

I'M SO THICK I BACKED WOGAN'S WINNER

Maureen's a maniokleptic – she walks backwards into shops and leaves things

MY DOG EATS ONIONS

HIS BARK IS FAR WORSE THAN HIS BITE

IRISH CARS SHOULD HAVE SILENT HORNS THEN THEY WOULDN'T DISTURB PEOPLE IN THE NIGHT

BALD IRISHMEN HAVE MORE HAIR THAN BRAINS

what happened to the Irishman who picked his nose for 100 years?

HIS FACE CAVED IN

BLOW YOUR MIND – EAT DYNAMITE

HEARD ABOUT THE IRISHMAN WHO PICKED HIS NOSE AND TORE THE LINING IN HIS HAT

SAVE PETROL THE
IRISH WAY — MAKE
ROADS SHORTER

ILLITERATE?
WRITE TODAY FOR FREE HELP

DYSLEXIC?
DAB CLUK

GO CLEAN ROUND THE BEND
DRINK HARPIC

SMOKE GRASS
AND GET TURFED
OUT OF YOUR MIND

MY INDIFFERENCE DOESN'T BOTHER ME

If a face can launch a thousand ships why do we waste good champagne?

When I hear the word WALL I reach for my magic marker

THERE'S FAR TOO MUCH APATHY IN THE WORLD, BUT THEN WHO CARES?

WHY GO TO A PSYCHIATRIST WHEN YOU CAN STAY AT HOME AND TALK TO THE CEILING FOR NOTHING?

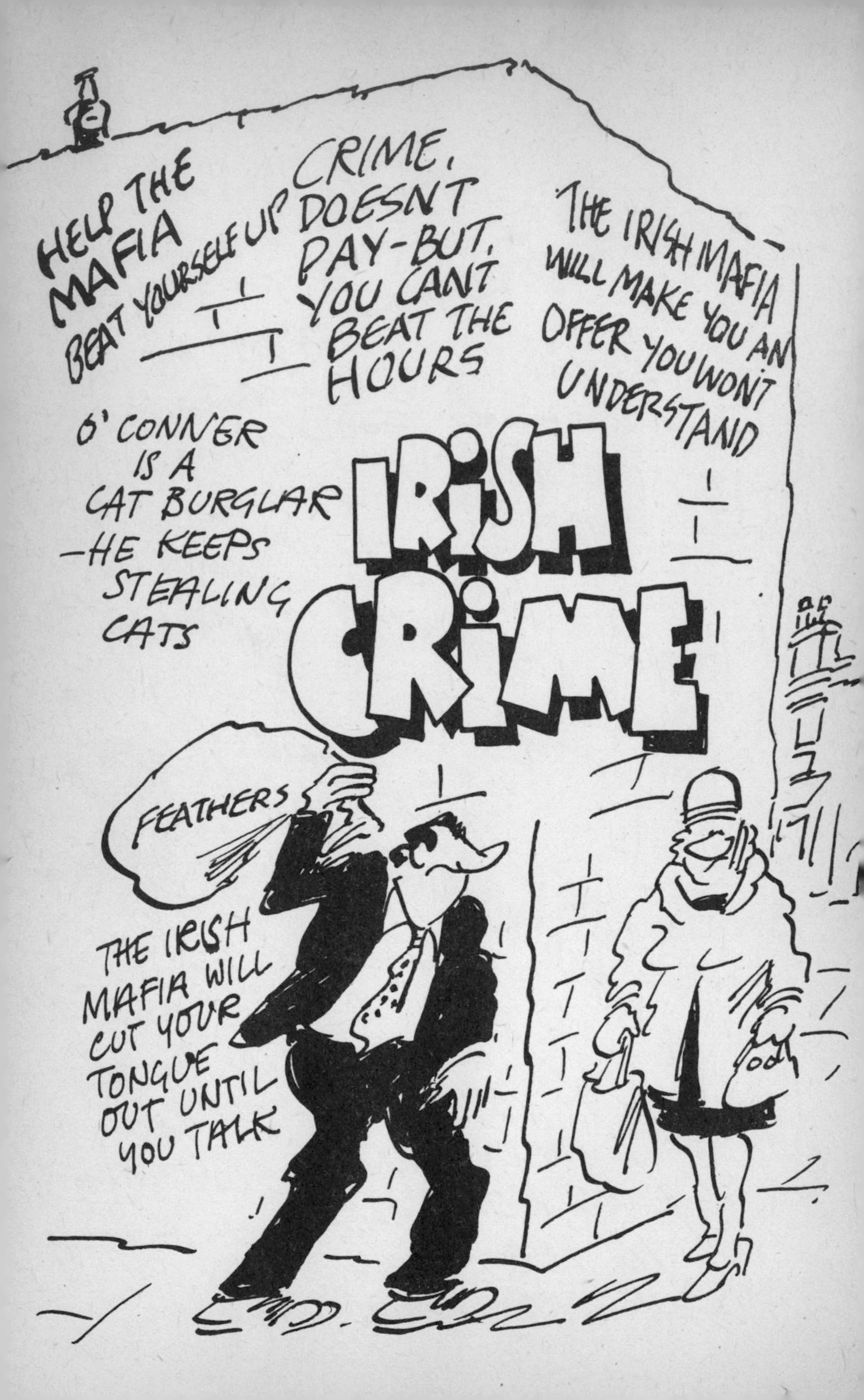
HELP THE MAFIA
BEAT YOURSELF UP
CRIME, DOESN'T PAY - BUT, YOU CAN'T BEAT THE HOURS
THE IRISH MAFIA WILL MAKE YOU AN OFFER YOU WON'T UNDERSTAND
O'CONNER IS A CAT BURGLAR - HE KEEPS STEALING CATS
IRISH CRIME
FEATHERS
THE IRISH MAFIA WILL CUT YOUR TONGUE OUT UNTIL YOU TALK

MURPHY TRIED TO BE A PICKPOCKET BUT HIS HANDS WERE TOO COLD

GRAFFITI IS AN EIGHT LETTER WORD.

Not the way I spell it! GRAFFEETEE

THE JUDGE GAVE ME 200 YEARS – I WAS LUCKY I DIDN'T GET LIFE

I DECIDED TO HAVE 30 DAYS IN JAIL RATHER THAN A MONTH.

My brother is a CRIMINAL LAWYER – AREN'T THEY ALL?

CRIME MAY NOT PAY BUT AT LEAST YOU'RE YOUR OWN BOSS

I got put inside for making BIG MONEY – about an INCH TOO BIG

MURPH GOT PUT INSIDE FOR FLAT FEET. HIS FEET WERE IN THE WRONG FLAT

At least being in prison
you're safe from
MUGGERS.

I WAS FOUND NOT GUILTY
OF BIGAMY, BUT THEN
I DIDN'T KNOW WHICH WIFE
TO GO HOME TO

I'M HERE FOR A TAX
OFFENCE

I MURDERED
THE VAT MAN

Give a man
enough rope
and he'll
hang you.

BE POPULAR
IN PRISON
BE THE LIFER
OF THE PARTY

DO NOT LEAN OUT
OF THIS WINDOW.

BRING BACK HANGING
-IT CURES CONSTIPATION

It stops you hanging
around in jail.

CLEENWALL

IRISH DRINK
GUINNESS
DARBY and JOAN CLUB
MURPHY SAVED ALL THE MONEY HE WOULD HAVE SPENT ON DRINK AND SPENT IT ON GUINNESS

WHY DOES GUINNESS HAVE A WHITE HEAD?
– SO YOU KNOW WHICH END TO DRINK FIRST
I drink therefore – I am
I'm drunk therefore I was..
I DRANK EIGHT COKES AND BURPED 7-UP
LIQUOR IS SLOW POISON – who's in a hurry?
DO YOU DO THE POOLS? NO, IT'S MY DOG
I've lost my glasses – WELL DRINK STRAIGHT FROM A BOTTLE
MY MONGREL HAS DISTEMPER
what do you expect with a mongrel CROWN GLOSS?

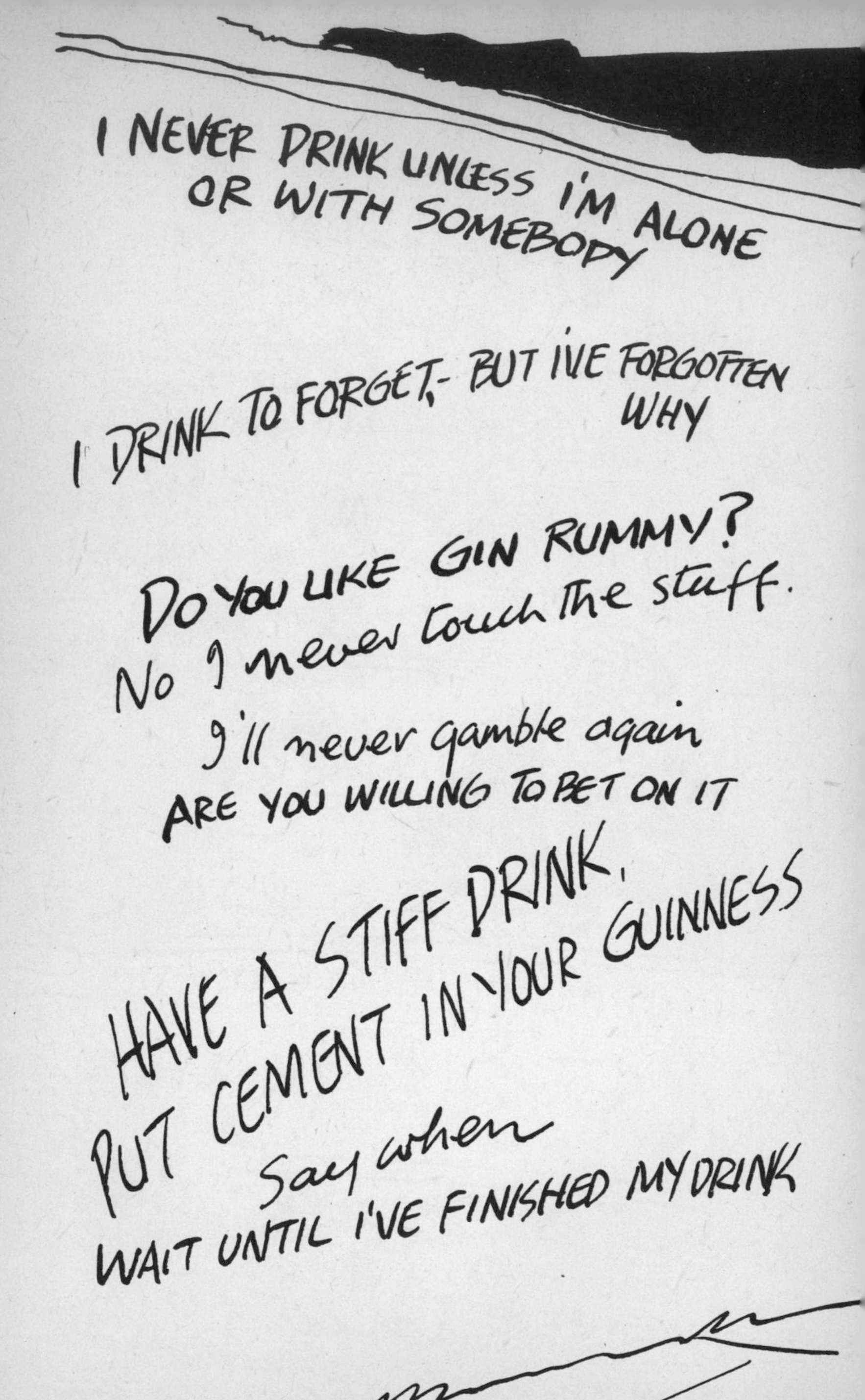
I NEVER DRINK UNLESS I'M ALONE OR WITH SOMEBODY
I DRINK TO FORGET,- BUT I'VE FORGOTTEN WHY
DO YOU LIKE GIN RUMMY?
No I never touch the stuff.
I'll never gamble again
ARE YOU WILLING TO BET ON IT
HAVE A STIFF DRINK,
PUT CEMENT IN YOUR GUINNESS
Say when
WAIT UNTIL I'VE FINISHED MY DRINK

ARE ALL THE IRISH BARTENDERS OF DOUBTFUL PARENTAGE?

MURPHY'S DOG IS DEAF
HE SHOUTED 'SIT'
AND NOW HE'S GOT TO
CLEAR THE MESS UP

The best
three things
of life
are a drunk
before
and a
cigarette
afterwards

DUBLIN
PISS
ARTISTES
RULE
O.K.

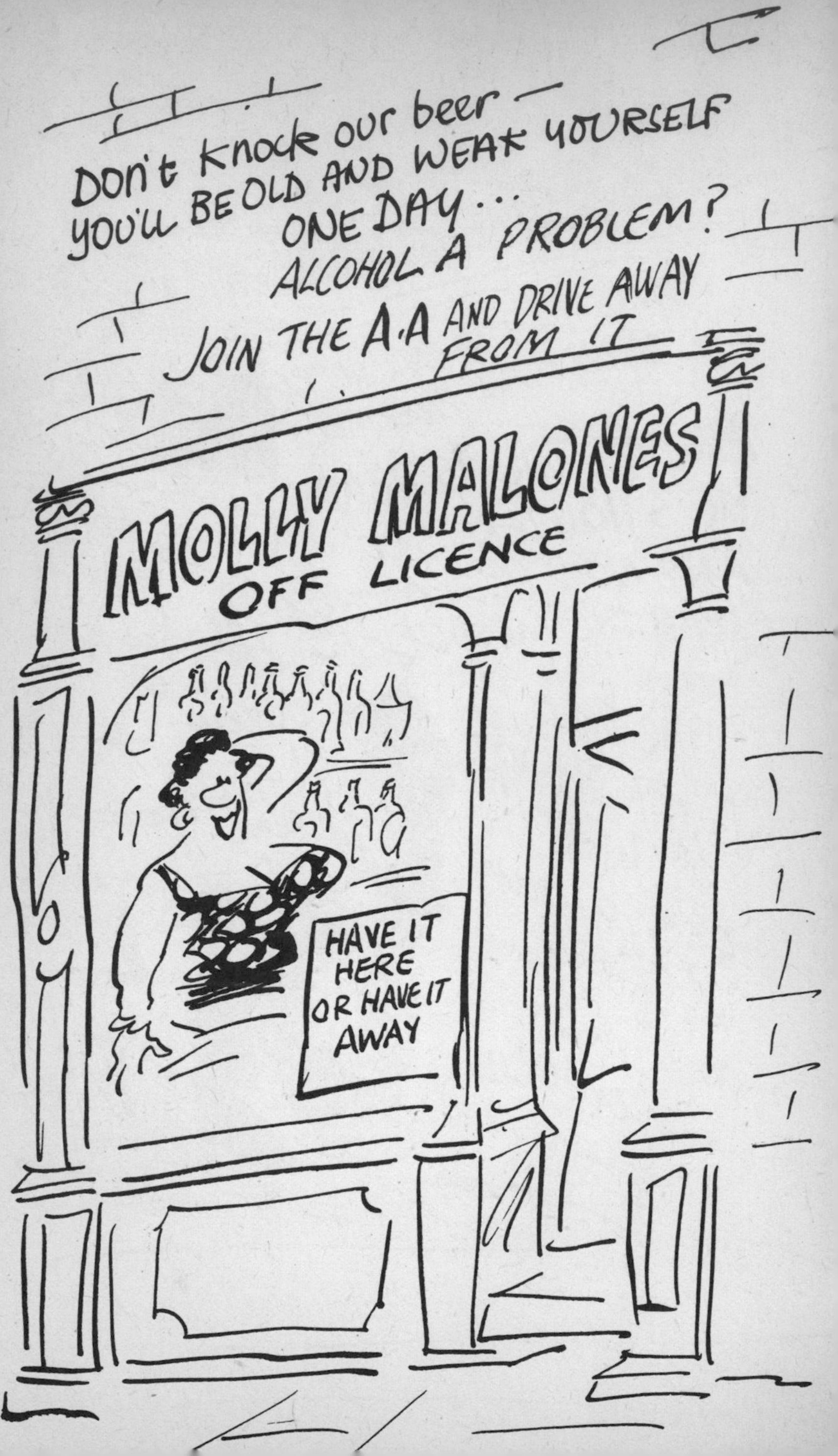

Don't knock our beer
YOU'LL BE OLD AND WEAK YOURSELF
ONE DAY...
ALCOHOL A PROBLEM?
JOIN THE A.A AND DRIVE AWAY
FROM IT

MOLLY MALONES
OFF LICENCE

HAVE IT
HERE
OR HAVE IT
AWAY

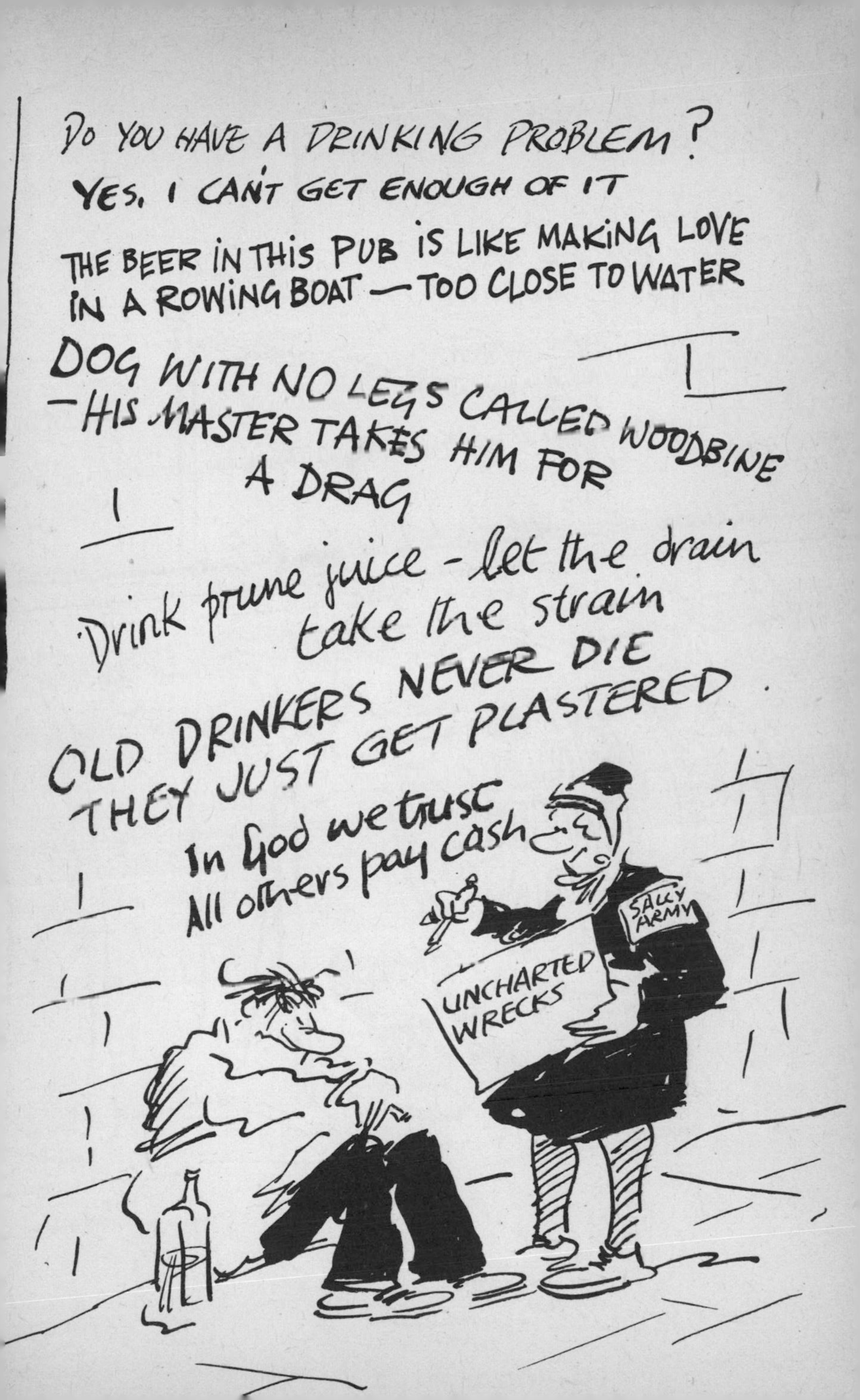
DO YOU HAVE A DRINKING PROBLEM?
YES. I CAN'T GET ENOUGH OF IT
THE BEER IN THIS PUB IS LIKE MAKING LOVE IN A ROWING BOAT — TOO CLOSE TO WATER
DOG WITH NO LEGS CALLED WOODBINE — HIS MASTER TAKES HIM FOR A DRAG
Drink prune juice - let the drain take the strain
OLD DRINKERS NEVER DIE THEY JUST GET PLASTERED
In God we trust All others pay cash
SALLY ARMY
UNCHARTED WRECKS

BOOZERS ARE LOSERS
DON'T TAKE THE PISS
OUT OF GUINNESS
IT NEEDS ALL THE FLAVOUR
IT CAN GET
REALITY IS A BOTTLE OF GUINNESS
I'M ASNISHED AS A PEWT
ONE MAN BAND
O'NELSON
FELL
HERE

MEN MAKE PASSES AT GIRLS
WHO DRAIN GLASSES
Don't drink and drive
It spills in your lap when
you change gear.
HAPPINESS IS IN CIDER ALL OF US.
DON'T DRIVE YOURSELF TO DRINK - GET A CHAUFFER
I'M NOT A STEADY DRINKER
No, your hand shakes too much.

IRISH EDUCATION
TRINITY COLLEGE DUBLIN
GENETICS
DEPARTMENT
TRESPASSERS WILL BE USED
TRINITY COLLEGE R.UFC
NEXT SATURDAYS FIXTURE
WILL BE PLAYED HERE ON
SUNDAY 17 JUNE
IRELAND

THE KIDS IN MY CLASS ARE SO TOUGH
THE TEACHERS PLAY TRUANT

LOOK AT AN IRISHMAN AND YOU'LL SEE
DARWIN WAS RIGHT

Wher do words go
when you rub them
off the black-Goard

I'VE GOT AN 'O' LEVEL IN WOODWORK

You can be an Irish BRAIN SURGEON

I've got 'O' levels in History and Woodwork
Can I make Antique Furniture?

QUASIMODO
THAT NAME
RINGS A BELL

READING
AND
RIOTING

MY PARENTS SENT ME
TO BOARDING SCHOOL
SO THEY WOULDN'T
HAVE TO HELP ME
WITH MY HOMEWORK

HISTORY
IS OUT
OF
DATE

I GOT A PRIZE FOR
PLAYING TRUANT
I WASN'T IN THE
SCHOOL PLAY

MURPHY IS THE TYPE
OF KID HIS MOTHER
TOLD HIM NOT TO
PLAY WITH

CLEANLINESS IS NEX TO GODLINESS
ONLY IN AN IRISH DICTIONARY
I WROTE THIS SLOW
'COS I KNOW YOU CAN'T
READ VERY FAST
O'REILLY GOT -1
IN HIS EXAM
HE SPELT HIS
NAME WRONG
I CAN'T SPELL
TCHIKOFSKI
I MAY BE
ILLITERATE
BUT AT
LEAST
I CAN
READ.

IF YOU CAN'T READ
WATCH THIS SPACE

WHEN I GROW UP
I WANT TO BE
PETER PAN
And I'll
be WINDY

CONVENT
OF
ST. DUMBROADS
ILLITERATE
ORDER

IGNORINSE
IS BUSS

AEROSOLS
TO
GRAFFITI

CHALKY
WHITE
TEACHER
GONE TO CRACK
SOME MORE SKULLS
UP ABOVE

BO-BEEP DID IT FOR THE INSURANCE

CINDERELLA MARRIED FOR MONEY

I BOUGHT THE TEACHER AN APPLE
AND SHE KISSED ME

Bring her a watermelon tomorrow

My mother made me a swot

HAS SHE GOT THE PATTERN SO THAT
I CAN MAKE ONE?

2B OR NOT 2B
OR SHOULD I USE A BIRO

A REPORT IS A POISON PEN LETTER WRITTEN
BY TEACHER.

CAREERS

(NO) THE HORSE KNACKER

CAFÉ DE PARIS

I'VE GOT A SOFT SPOT
FOR MY TEACHER
– A BOG IN
NORTHERN IRELAND

If all teachers
are in loco-parentis
The ones at our
School must be
imposters

MUSICIANS
DO IT
BY THE
SCORE

MATRICULATION
MAKES YOU
DEAF
PARDON?

KEEP FIT CLASSES
CANCELLED
DUE TO ILNESS.

IRISH FOOD
CANNIBAL FOOD BAR
TODAYS SPECIAL
BROTH
OF A
BOY
IRISH FOOD IS GREAT
FOR PIGS

WHY DOESN'T SOYA MEAT HAVE BONES?

The best way to serve leftovers – give them to someone else

I LIKE MAKING MUD PIES

HOPE YOU WASH YOUR HANDS BEFORE YOU EAT THEM

FANCY A BITE? DRACULA

I'm a sucker for punishment.

I'M IN A HURRY – JUST BRING ME THE BILL

SALIVA DROOLS O.K.

ALL DRINKING WATER HERE IS PASSED BY THE MANAGEMENT

MICK'S CAFÉ

FOOD FOR O.A.P's HALF PRICE AND HALF COOKED

NEVER EAT ON EMPTY STONIACH
MY WIFE'S GOT A FRENCH COOKBOOK. SHE CAN'T READ FRENCH BUT THE WAY SHE COOKS IT DOESN'T MATTER
The less people know about how sausages are made, the better they'll sleep at night
I WANTED HUNGARIAN STEW BUT THE BUTCHER HAD RUN OUT OF HUNGARIANS
THE GREAT IRISH POTATO FAMINE
JACKET POTATOES £2·50p

IRISH WAY OF PREVENTING RICE FROM STICKING TOGETHER: BOIL EACH GRAIN SEPERATELY
EVERYTHING COMES TO HE WHO ORDERS IRISH STEW
AVOID COOKING SMELLS IN THE KITCHEN. STOP COOKING.
HOW DO YOU COOK A SMELL ANYWAY?
I'M FED UP WITH PLANNING MEALS
Kick the shelf in Tescos and take whatever falls off
IRISH RAILBAR
GASTRIC JUICE
MAKE CUCUMBERS LOOK LIKE BANANAS BUY SOME YELLOW PAINT
I DON'T KNOW WHAT TO MAKE OF MY HUSBAND
HOW ABOUT MINCEMEAT?

DON'T VOTE, THE GOVERNMENT WILL GET IN

IRISH GOVERNMENT

I'M A SELF-MADE MAN

We accept your apology

GOV'T IS A NASTY FOUR LETTER WORD

If you don't vote for me - I'll hold my breath

MEN LIKE HIM ARE A DYING BREED WHO WILL LIVE FOREVER

FREE IRELAND

FROM THE IRISH

ARE YOU IN LABOUR?

No, it's not due for another fortnight

IN THIS WORLD YOU'VE GOT TO BE CRAZY OR YOU WOULD GO MAD

BLACK

TAN

I LIKE LISTENING TO THE WOODENTOPS
YES, I LIKE QUESTION TIME IN IRISH PARLIAMENT TOO
WITH THE GOVERNMENT THESE DAYS A MAN CAN'T AFFORD TO MAE A LIVING
IF IRISH POLITICIANS WERE LAID END TO END THEY'D HAVE THEIR FEET IN EACH OTHERS MOUTHS
BALLOT BOX
Mrs Thatcher is a LESBIAN. Denise Thatcher

THERE'S NO PLACE LIKE IRELAND
THANK GOD!

THE IRISH PRIME MINISTER DOES THE WORK OF TWO MEN
LAUREL AND HARDY

DON'T VOTE – IT ONLY ENCOURAGES THEM.

I NEVER GET LOST – EVERYBODY TELLS ME WHERE TO GO

Join the IRISH COMMUNIST PARTY

SANTA CLAUS IS A COMMUNIST – THAT'S WHY HE ALWAYS WEARS RED.

THE PRIME MINISTER UNDERSTANDS THE QUESTIONS OF THE DAY
BUT DOESN'T KNOW THE ANSWERS

The government is clever. They raise the price of drink, then make sure the country is in such a mess that you drink more.

I'd vote for Oliver Cromwell if I thought it would do the country any good.

IRISH HOBBIES
GUINNESS
GUINNESS
GUINNESS
GUINNESS
GUINNESS
GUINNESS
GUINNESS
GUINNES
GUINNESS
GUINNESS
GUINNESS
GUINNESS
DRIPMAT COLLECTORS WORLD
HOUDINI WAS JUST AN ILLUSION
FRIGHTEN YOURSELF RIGID
MAKE A PARACHUTE JUMP

IRISH PARTY GAME
PIN THE HORNS ON THE DOINKEY
I'M A TINKER
OH! AND WHAT ARE YOU TINKING ABOUT
I like to have a useful hobby like walking down the up escalator
STAMP OUT FLAMENCO DANCING
JOGGERS OF THE WORLD UNITE
YOU'VE GOT NOTHING TO LOSE BUT THE SOLES OF YOUR SHOES
O'LEGGO
HOBBY SHOP
SOFT TOY MAKING
WHISKEY DISTILLING
IRISH MOTH SPOTTING
POPEOPOLY
D.O.Y GRAVE DIGGING
PAINT SPRAYING HERE
EASY TO DO JIG SAW 3 PIECES
LEATHERWORK
STAMP COLLECTING
HEAD BANGING
TAKING DRUGS IS JUST LIKE A BOWL OF CHERRIES — SOONER OR LATER YOU GET STONED

DO YOU LIKE DICKENS?
I dont know I've never been to one.
MOST POPULAR IRISH HOBBY- COLLECTING DUST
IRISHMEN GET TENNIS ELBOW PLAYING TIDDLY-WINKS
my favourite game is pin the tail on the donkey.
BET YOU HAVE A SORE ASS FOR A WEEK AFTERWARDS.
PHOTOGRAPHS DON'T DO ME JUSTICE
IT'S MERCY YOU WANT NOT JUSTICE
THE VATICAN SOUVENIR PHOTOGRAPHS

IRISH FOOTBALL GAMES HAVE MORE GOALS THAN FANS.

THE IRISH HERNIA SOCIETY NEEDS YOUR SUPPORT

GONE FISSION

CAGED BIRDS SOCIETY

1982 SHOW

The Nolan sisters are tops — despite their knockers.

ENJOY YOURSELF — RUN OVER A TRAFFIC WARDEN TODAY

WOMEN LIKE THE SIMPLE THINGS IN LIFE — Like Irishmen

BEST IN SHOW MEDAL (POSTHUMOUS)

IRISH IDEAS
TINKS
LATEST IRISH INVENTION EJECTOR SEAT FOR HELICOPTERS.
A POEM

Why do birthday suits only have one button

AVOID ROAD TAX "DRIVE ON THE PAVEMENT"

IRISH ICE-CREAM MELTS IN THE FRIDGE

I'D LIKE TO BUMP OFF DOLLY PARTON

Don't you mean knock off

I KNOW WHAT I MEAN

SAVE MONEY ON LAMPS – MINE COAL DURING THE DAY

Isn't Dolly Parton a lovely pair?

IF IT WASN'T FOR VENETIAN BLINDS IT WOULD BE CURTAINS FOR ALL OF US!

Why don't astronauts Go and land on the sun

IRISH TREETS MELT IN THE PACKET NOT IN YOUR HAND

PATENTS OFFICE

NO, THEY MELT IN YOUR MOUTH NOT IN YOUR SHOVEL

PATENT BOTTLE OPENER

HEATH D'ROBINSON

IRISH INSECTICIDES KILL THE CROPS SO THAT INSECTS STARVE TO DEATH
COMMIT SUICIDE THE IRISH WAY - SLIP ARSENIC IN YOUR TEA WHILE YOU LOOK THE OTHER WAY
why don't they have a radio phone-in for the deaf
WHY DON'T THEY MAKE SAUCEPAN'S LONG ENOUGH TO COOK SPAGHETTI?
Why do chickens eat only Sage and Onion?
YOU CAN TELL THE AGE OF AN ONION BY COUNTING THE RINGS
THE IRISH INVENT THE WHEEL 1792

MUNSTER MUNCH
CRISPS LTD

SMOKING SHORTENS YOUR CIGARETTES

BETWEEN AN IRISHMAN'S EYES
IS SOMETHING THAT SMELLS

EVERY DOG HAS ITS DAY, BUT
ONLY A DOG WITH A BROKEN
TAIL HAS A WEAK-END.

IF YESTERDAY WAS TODAY – TODAY
WOULD BE YESTERDAY

If music be the food
of love, why dont
rabbits play banjos

THE SILENT CRISP

COTTON
WOOL

COTTON
WOOL

IRISHMEN LOVE EVERYBODY
You have been warned
TERRY WOGAN RULES O. BLANK
Life is a myth
SO IS TERRY WOGAN
ALL ENGLISHMEN ARE DAFT
YES. DAFT ENOUGH TO PUT UP WITH YOU IRISH
IRISHMEN SMELL SO THAT BLIND PEOPLE CAN HATE THEM TOO
IRISH WOLFHOUNDS FOR THE BLIND
YOUR GUINNESS NEEDS YOU

FLASH GORDON INVENTED THE ZIP.
PILES ARE NATURES WAY OF SAYING YOU ARE A LAZY GIT
CLEAN UP DUBLIN EAT A TOURIST
CUPID WENT BLIND BY THE HAND OF FATE
OLD HOLBORN
FEET ROLLING TOBACCO ON SALE NOW
MOTHER KELLY'S DOORSTEP

IRISH
JOBS

JOB
CENTAUR

I SELL PROGRAMMES AT CORONATIONS - THE MONEY'S NOT GOOD BUT THE HOURS ARE GREAT
DID YOU HEAR ABOUT THE IRISH TUBE TRAIN DRIVER WHO WAS SACKED FOR OVERTAKING
BERNARD MANNING THINK HE'S WORTH £1,000 A PERFORMANCE
That's the funniest joke he's ever told
A PERFECT WORLD SHOULD HAVE A SIX DAY WEEK-END
I USED TO BE A GLASS BLOWER BUT IT GAVE ME A PANE
NCP
I'M ONLY HERE FOR THE BIER
O'DEATH FUNERAL DIRECTORS
TAKE ONE FOR YOUR FRIEND

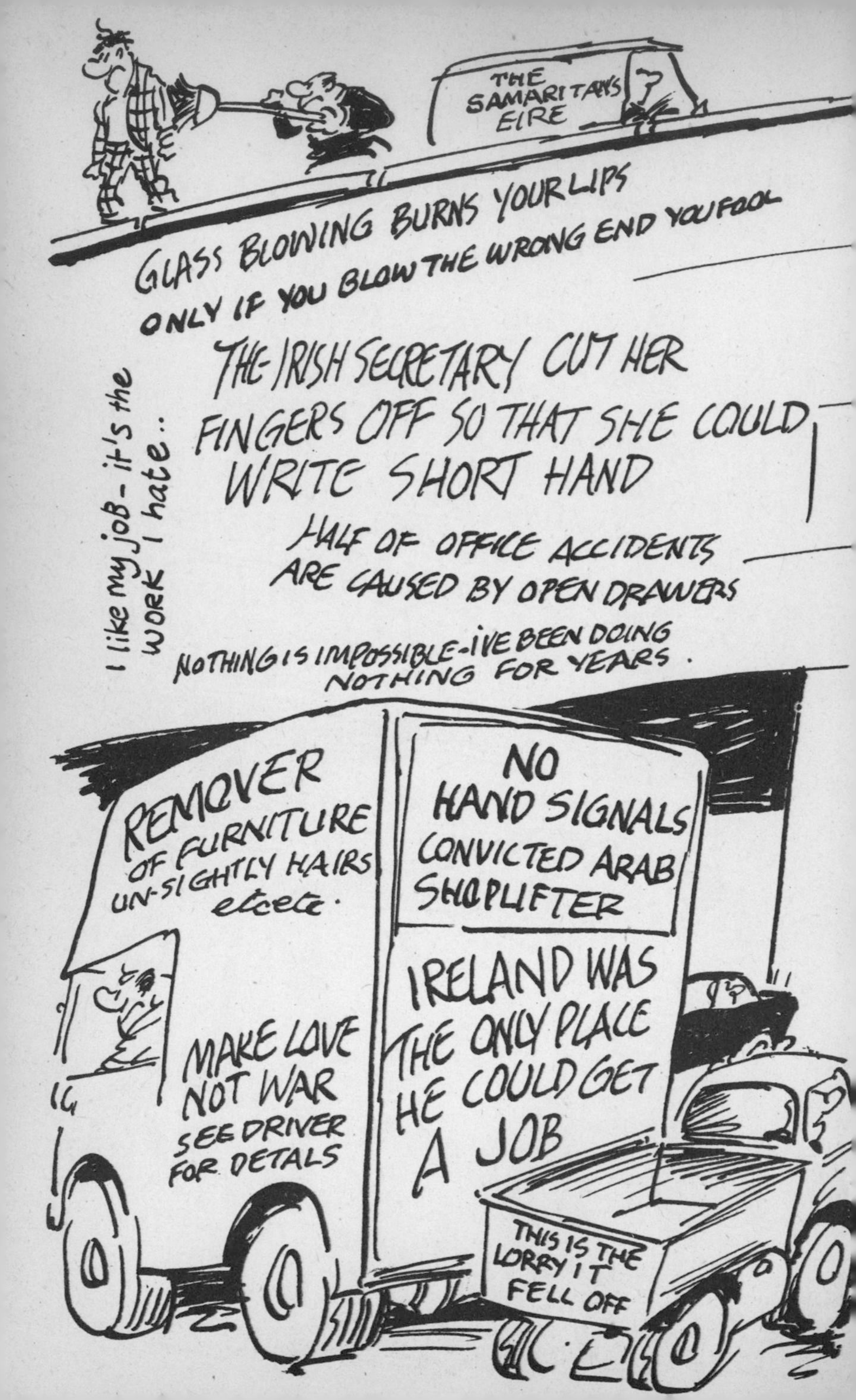
THE SAMARITANS EIRE
GLASS BLOWING BURNS YOUR LIPS
ONLY IF YOU BLOW THE WRONG END YOU FOOL
THE IRISH SECRETARY CUT HER FINGERS OFF SO THAT SHE COULD WRITE SHORT HAND
HALF OF OFFICE ACCIDENTS ARE CAUSED BY OPEN DRAWERS
NOTHING IS IMPOSSIBLE - IVE BEEN DOING NOTHING FOR YEARS.
I like my job - it's the work I hate..
REMOVER OF FURNITURE UN-SIGHTLY HAIRS etcetc.
NO HAND SIGNALS
CONVICTED ARAB SHOPLIFTER
IRELAND WAS THE ONLY PLACE HE COULD GET A JOB
MAKE LOVE NOT WAR
SEE DRIVER FOR DETALS
THIS IS THE LORRY IT FELL OFF

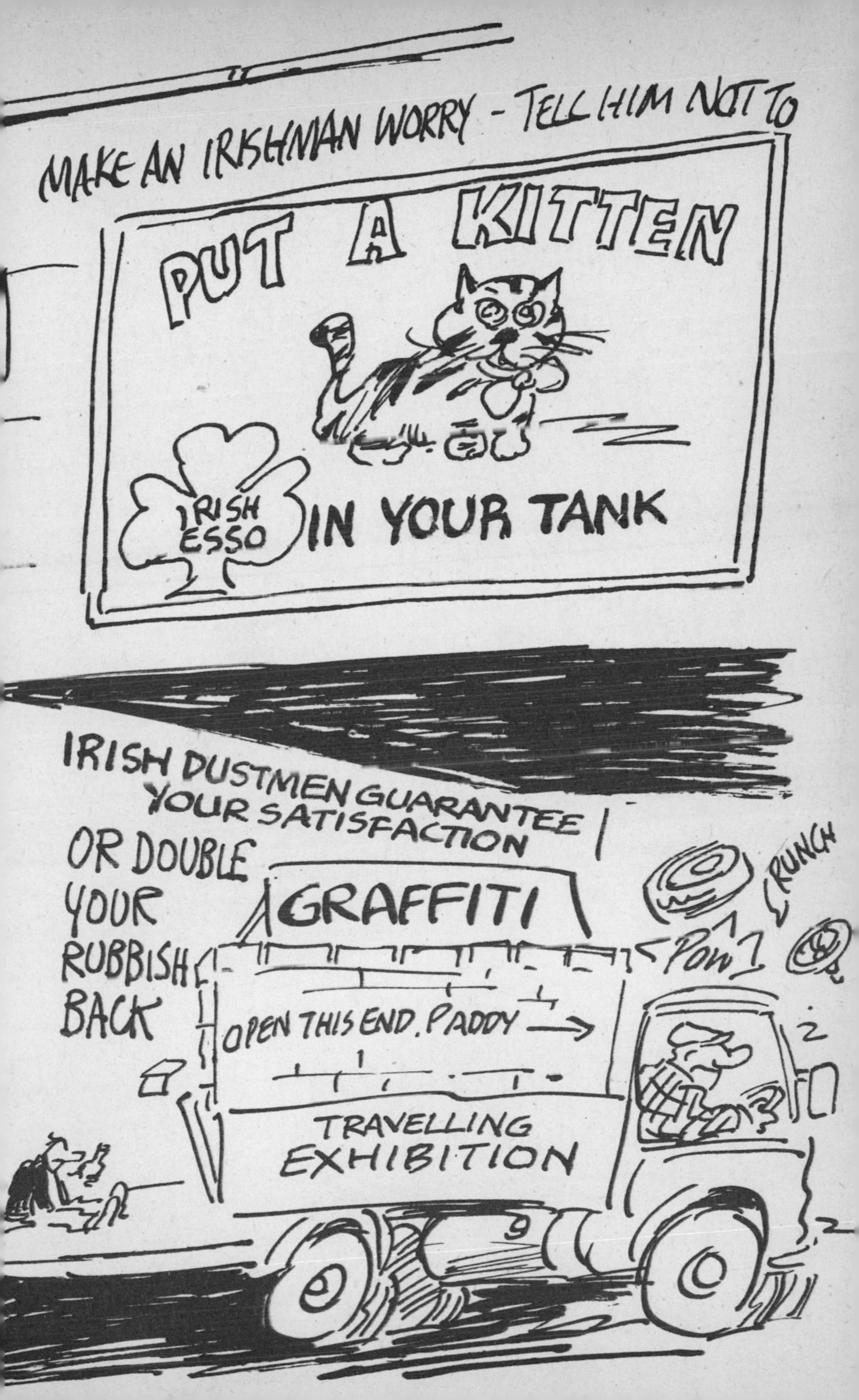
MAKE AN IRISHMAN WORRY - TELL HIM NOT TO
PUT A KITTEN
IRISH ESSO
IN YOUR TANK
IRISH DUSTMEN GUARANTEE YOUR SATISFACTION
OR DOUBLE YOUR RUBBISH BACK
GRAFFITI
OPEN THIS END, PADDY
TRAVELLING EXHIBITION
POW
CRUNCH

EARN CASH IN YOUR SPARE TIME BLACKMAIL YOUR FRIENDS

IRISH COMEDIANS STEAL JOKES FROM BERNARD MANNING

I WANT TO PLAY THE TITLE ROLE IN WAITING FOR GODOT

MY STEAM-ROLLER'S GOT A PUNCTURE

I DRIVE A SNOWPLOUGH BUT ONLY IN THE SUMMER

PLEASE PASS DRIVER ON OVERTIME

DRIVER SUFFERING FROM BOTTLE FATIGUE

NO HAND SIGNALS DRIVER FROM IRELAND

What is a Yorkie IT'S A DOG

YOU CAN TELL AN 'IRISH' WORKMAN BY HIS HANDS
TO AIR IS HUMAN - TO FORKLIFT IS DIVINE
PLAY STREET
REDUNDANT WORKERS ONLY
THEY'RE ALWAYS RESTING ON HIS SHOVEL
COBBLERS TO THE GENTRY
JOB CREATION SCHEME FIRE BRIGADE
HOP SCOTCH
HIDE AND SEEK

IRISH KITH
MURPHY
MURPHY
MURPHY
MURP
MORE MURPHYS
MURPHY
MURPHY
MURPHY
MURPHY
MURPHY
MURPHY
GIVE ME A KITH, I WITH YOU WOULDN'T RUTH ME
I'VE HAD TEN CHILDREN
WELL, THE KIDS NEEDED A MOTHER

MOUNTAINS OF MOURN TO THE SEA

I'VE GOT TWO SONS – BOTH BOYS

BRIDGET WENT WINDOW SHOPPING CAME BAK WITH 17 WINDOWS

There were 20 in my family I never slept alone until I was married

I'M GOING TO RUN AWAY FROM HOME AS SOON AS WE GET ONE

MY MOTHER WAS A FAN DANCER UNTIL SHE GOT ELECTROCUTED BY ONE

DID YOU HEAR ABOUT THE IRISH HOUSEWIFE WHO SHOT HER HUSBAND WITH A BOW AND ARROW? SHE DIDN'T WANT TO WAKE THE CHILDREN

SUCCESS IS RELATIVE
THE MORE SUCCESS THE MORE RELATIVES

I THOUGHT YOU WERE YOURSELF. BUT NOW I'VE GOT MY GLASSES ON I CAN SEE YOU ARE YOUR BROTHER

HOME SWEET HOME

MY SON WASN'T BROUGHT BY A STORK, BUT BY A LARK IN THE FIELD.

self portrait

SHE WAS ONLY THE CARPENTERS DAUGHTER, BUT SHE WOOD.

CHILDREN SHOULD BE SEEN AND NOT HAD.

QUICK BRING A HAMMER. THERE'S A FLY ON THE BABIES HEAD.

My mother in law is a real treasure wish it was buried.

GRADIENT 1 IN 1

THE RAILWAY KIDS

I DON'T LIKE AUNT BRIDGET
AM I ANTI-AUNTIE?

DON'T SHOUT AT ME
I'M NOT YOUR MOTHER

Murphy shot both his parents so that he could go to the orphans picnic

HAVE THE NOLAN SISTERS GOT A BROTHER?
HE'S THE ONE IN THE MIDDLE

ARE WE DESCENDED FROM MONKEYS?
I DON'T KNOW I NEVER MET YOUR FATHER'S PEOPLE

BEAUTY | THE BEAST

IRISH LUCK
BINGO

BAD LUCK IS BENDING OVER TO PICK UP A FOUR LEAF CLOVER AND BEING INFECTED WITH POISON IVY

ALL BRAN MAKES ME CONSTIPATED

My egg-timer is fast

MURPHY'S SWIMMING POOL BROKE DOWN

A fate worse than death is better than dying

Rennies give me indigestion

I FINALLY GOT IT ALTOGETHER THEN I FORGOT WHERE I PUT IT

I HAVE TO COUNT SHEEP TO KEEP AWAKE

THINK YOU'VE GOT TROUBLES?
MY SUN-DIAL IS SLOW

WHY IS IT THE ONE
THAT SNORES IS THE
ONE THAT FALLS ASLEEP
FIRST

I WENT BALD
AT PUBERTY

I HAVEN'T HAD SEX SINCE 1956
Well it's only 2330 now

A STITCH IN
TIME SAVES
AN EMBARRASSING
EXPOSURE

Heard about the
Irishman who took his
girl out into the fog
and mist?

NEWS
CORK MAN SHOULD
HAVE HAD POOLS WIN
WORTH £635,780
BUT FORGOT TO
POST COUPON

DADDY LOST HIS HANDS
I wonder how he
feels

MY
ARMPITS
HAVE
SPLIT ENDS

I DON'T EXPECT THE WORST
I DEPEND ON IT
Be pessimistic
IF EVOLUTION WORKED
WE'D HAVE MORE THAN
ONE PAIR OF HANDS
stamp on your cigarette
before asking if
anyones got a light
FOR SUCCESS — PLAN AHE
IRISH SCHOOL OF MOTORING
L
DRIVING
TEST
FAIL

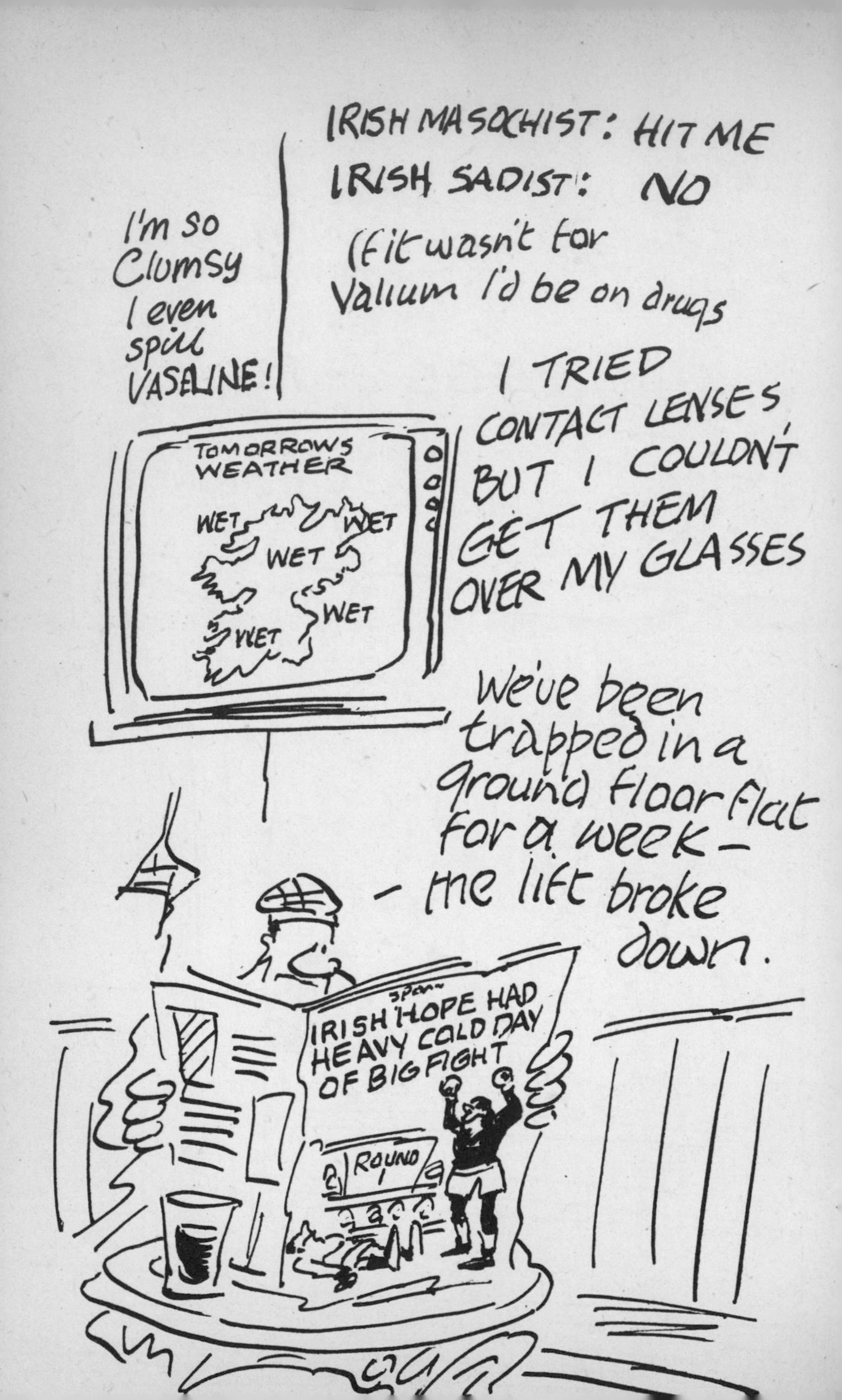
IRISH MASOCHIST: HIT ME
IRISH SADIST: NO
I'm so Clumsy I even spill VASELINE!
If it wasn't for Valium I'd be on drugs
I TRIED CONTACT LENSES BUT I COULDN'T GET THEM OVER MY GLASSES
TOMORROWS WEATHER
WET
WET
WET
WET
WET
We've been trapped in a ground floor flat for a week - - the lift broke down.
IRISH HOPE HAD HEAVY COLD DAY OF BIG FIGHT
ROUND 1

I never used to be able to finish anything but now I

IRISH MARRIAGE
HAVE A SHORT WIFE AND A MERRY ONE
Generally speaking my wife is
AA
JUST MARRIED
AA IRELAND
AA
I'VE BEEN MARRIED 12 MONTHS, BUT IT SEEMS MORE LIKE A YEAR TO ME

MURPHY'S WIFE HAD TRIPLETS NOW HE'S TRYING TO FIND OUT WHO THE OTHER TWO BLOKES ARE.
My wife got a grant to go to weight-watchers
MARRIAGE IS GIVE AND TAKE
Yeh, I give and she takes
MURPHY'S WIFE IS SO UGLY, AT THE WEDDING EVERYONE KISSED HIM.
AND THEY SAID THE MARRIAGE WOULDN'T LAST. THEY LEFT THE CHURCH TOGETHER DIDN'T THEY?
MARRIAGE ISN'T A WORD IT'S A SENTENCE
IF YOUR WIFE DOESN'T FANCY YOU, TRY MAKING LOVE TO HER DAILY
FOOT MOUTH

I BOUGHT MY WIFE A TOILET BRUSH BUT SHE DIDN'T LIKE IT. WE'VE GONE BACK TO USING PAPER
im very happily divorced.
Divorce costs more than marriage, but it's worth every penny
CONTRACEPTIVES SHOULD BE USED ON EVERY CONCEIVABLE OCCASION
MY WIFE IS SO SHORT SIGHTED SHE CAN'T TELL IF IT'S A MAN UNLESS HE'S RIGHT ON TOP OF HER.
MRS. MURPHY GOT MARRIED IN CURLERS SHE WANTED TO LOOK NICE AT THE RECEPTION.
WHA'A STAG PARTY LAST NIGHT!

SMART MEN MAKE GOOD HUSBANDS
SMART MEN DON'T GET MARRIED
MEN WHO MARRY WOMEN ARE FOOLS!
But who else can they marry?
WELL, I'M FREE
MARRYING A WOMAN FOR BEAUTY IS LIKE BUYING A HOUSE FOR ITS PAINT
yeh. it soon peels off

IRISH NOTICES
TELEPHONE
TELEPHONE
THERE WILL BE A MEETING FOR ALL VIRGINS IN THIS PHONE BOX AT 6.00pm
What's a virgin?
I DON'T THINK I EVER WAS ONE
WAITING LIMITED TO 60 MINUTES IN ANY HOUR
THIS LIFT DOESN'T WORK
KEEP IRELAND TIDY
THROW YOUR RUBBISH AWAY

HAPPINESS IS CONTAGIOUS
BE A CARRIER

EAT PRUNES AND START
A MOVEMENT

KEEP DEATH OFF
THE ROADS, DRIVE
ON THE PAVEMENT

FEELING LONELY?
LOOK ME UP IN THE
YELLOW PAGES
or ring
BELFAST 823239.

IF YOU WANT A SCREW GO TO AN IRONMONGERS
OR RING BELFAST 823239.

OLD-LANG SIGNS LTD

Mc SEX
NOT
WAR

SCOTTISH
GRAFFITI
CATERED
FOR

EARS
PIERCED
WHILE
U
WAIT

JONES BATTERY FARM
GET NEWLY LAID
DOWN THE YARD
Dear Milkman
NO MILK TODAY
IF THIS LETTER
BLOWS AWAY
PLEASE KNOCK
ON THE DOOR
CAUTION
SUDDEN
TEA BREAKS
GAS
BOARD
BRAMLEY
MATERNITY HOSPITAL
THIS IS NOT AN
ACCIDENT UNIT
TAKE ADVANTAGE
OF YOUR MILKMAN
HE WON'T MIND
A BIT
MURPHY
UNDERTAKERS
PARKING
FOR
REGULAR
CUSTOMERS
ONLY

NO SMOKING
GUIDE DOGS EXCEPTED
PLEASE DO NOT USE THE LIFT WHEN IT IS NOT WORKING
OUT TO LUNCH IF NOT BACK BY 3 O'CLOCK FLAT OUT
CLOSING DOWN: THANKS TO ALL OUR CUSTOMERS
AUTOMATIC WASHERS
PLEASE REMOVE ALL YOUR CLOTHES WHEN THE LIGHT GOES OUT
THIS STAIRCASE IS IN A DANGEROUS CONDITION – IT WILL BE CLOSED AT THE END OF THE TOURIST SEASON

GAR
LAST GARAGE BEFORE NEXT ONE
DENTACAR HIRE
DANGER!!!
TO TOUCH THESE WIRES MEANS CERTAIN DEATH
ANYONE DISREGARDING THIS NOTICE WILL BE PROSECUTED
BRAHMS LIZT
PLEASE LEAVE CLEAR THE GAS COMPANY ARE COMING
SO IS CHRISTMAS WATCH THIS SPACE TO SEE WHO ARRIVES FIRST
ROAD HOG

KILKENNY
WOMEN'S CLUB
TONIGHTS TALK:
DID YOU KNOW THAT THE
FIRST FEW MINUTES OF
HUMAN LIFE ARE OFTEN
THE MOST DANGEROUS?
The last few
can be a bit
dodgy too!
ROWNTREES
LION BAR
BITE IT, CRUNCH IT
CHEW IT
Then stuff it
down your throat
IF THIS IS
SEX
IT SOUNDS
LIKE FUN
DOES THIS LETTER
BELONG TO YOU?
THE NAME IS
SMUDGED.
NO, MY NAME
IS O'GRADY
THE
WORLD
WILL END
ON FRIDAY
I WASN'T PLANNING
ON DOING ANYTHING
AT THE
WEEK-END
ANYWAY

J. P. O'NEILL LISch
CHIROPODIST
AND IRISH
BRAIN SURGEON
DONEGAL
SATURDAY NIGHT
DANCE
VERY EXCLUSIVE
ALL WELCOME
BOOK EARLY TO
BE SURE OF
DISAPPOINTMENT
VISIT THE
IRISH POST OFFICE
TOWER
The restaurant stands still
The diners run round in circles.
THERE WILL BE
NO MORE NOTICES
UNTIL FURTHER
NOTICE
THIS IS NOT
A CONTRACEPTIVE
MACHINE
KILROYS
DOG WAS
HERE

NO ADMITTANCE UNLESS YOU WANT TO COME IN
WET PAINT
YOURE RIGHT!
LIFT
DO NOT USE LIFT IN CASE OF FIRE JUST JUMP
NO SMOKING ALLOWED
PLEASE SMOKE QUIETLY
SPEAK WHEN YOU HEAR THE GREEN LIGHT
PHONE DEAD
BURIAL ON FRIDAY
WRITE YOUR NAME ON BOTH SIDES OF A LUGGAGE LABEL IN CASE IT COMES OFF
AER LINGUS

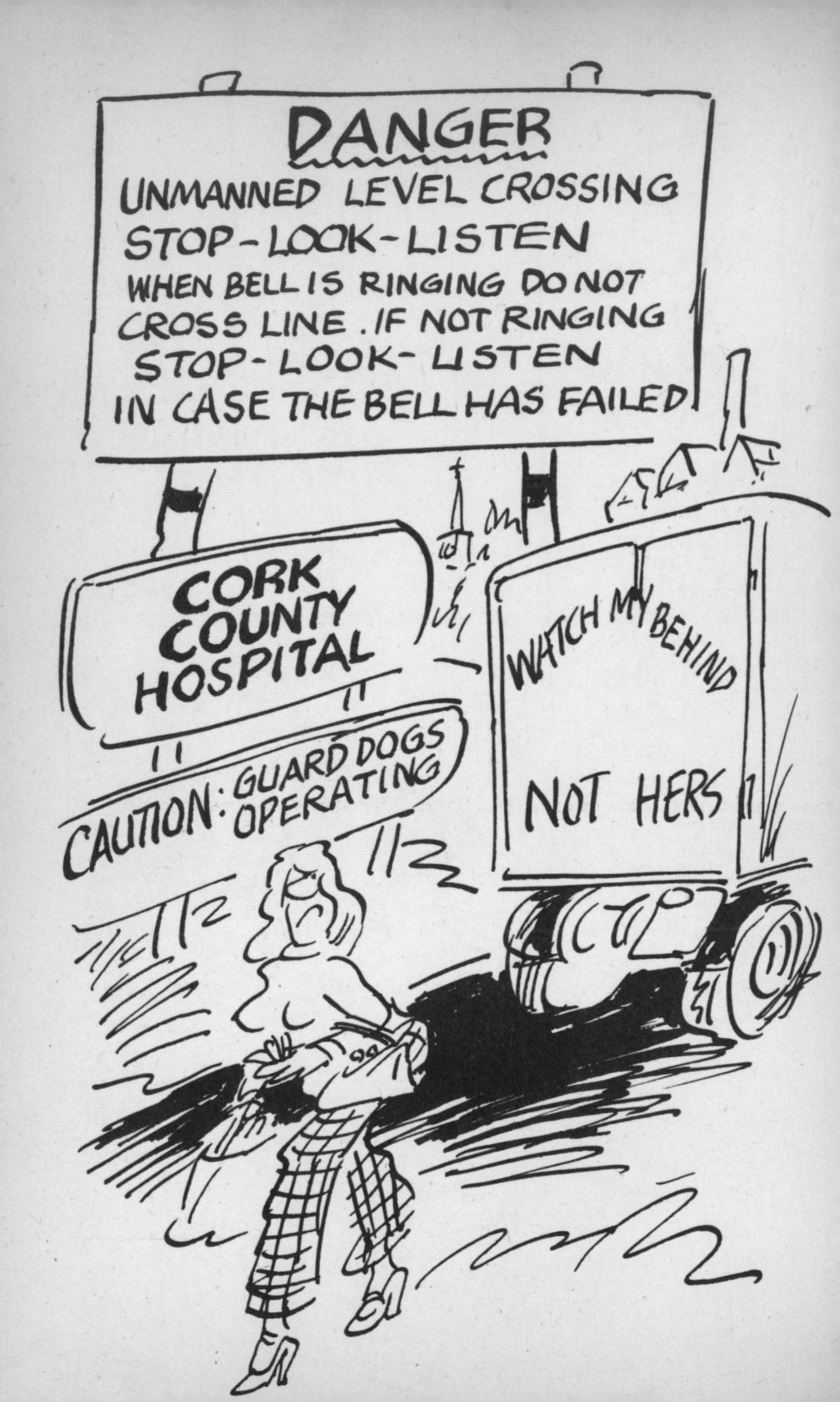
DANGER
UNMANNED LEVEL CROSSING
STOP-LOOK-LISTEN
WHEN BELL IS RINGING DO NOT
CROSS LINE. IF NOT RINGING
STOP-LOOK-LISTEN
IN CASE THE BELL HAS FAILED
CORK COUNTY HOSPITAL
CAUTION: GUARD DOGS OPERATING
WATCH MY BEHIND
NOT HERS

BRING YOUR CHILDREN TO CORK
AND LEAVE THE LITTLE BASTARDS THERE
AVENUE ROAD
What's wrong with the old one then?
TRAIN SPOTTERS GUIDE
PLEASE LEAVE ONE GATE OPEN
WE'RE HALF EXPECTING A TRAIN

USE NON CURL POSTER PAPER

NOTHING BEATS THE GREAT SMELL OF BRUT

I'LL USE NOTHING THEN

USE BAH GUM.

CONFERENCE ON SCHIZOPHRENIA

THE ANNUAL CONFERENCE FOR IRISH CLAIRVOYANTS HAS BEEN CANCELLED DUE TO UNFORSEEN CIRCUMSTANCES

I've half a mind to go.

SAY IT WITH FLOWERS

Hit her over the head with a bouquet

I've got a hole in my bouquet

WELL USE A PAIL THEN

FRESH EIRE

PICK YOUR OWN MANURE

FOUND ONE PAIR OF GLASSES
PLEASE WRITE LARGER
I'VE LOST MY GLASSES

IRISH
OPINION

IRISH GALLOP POLE

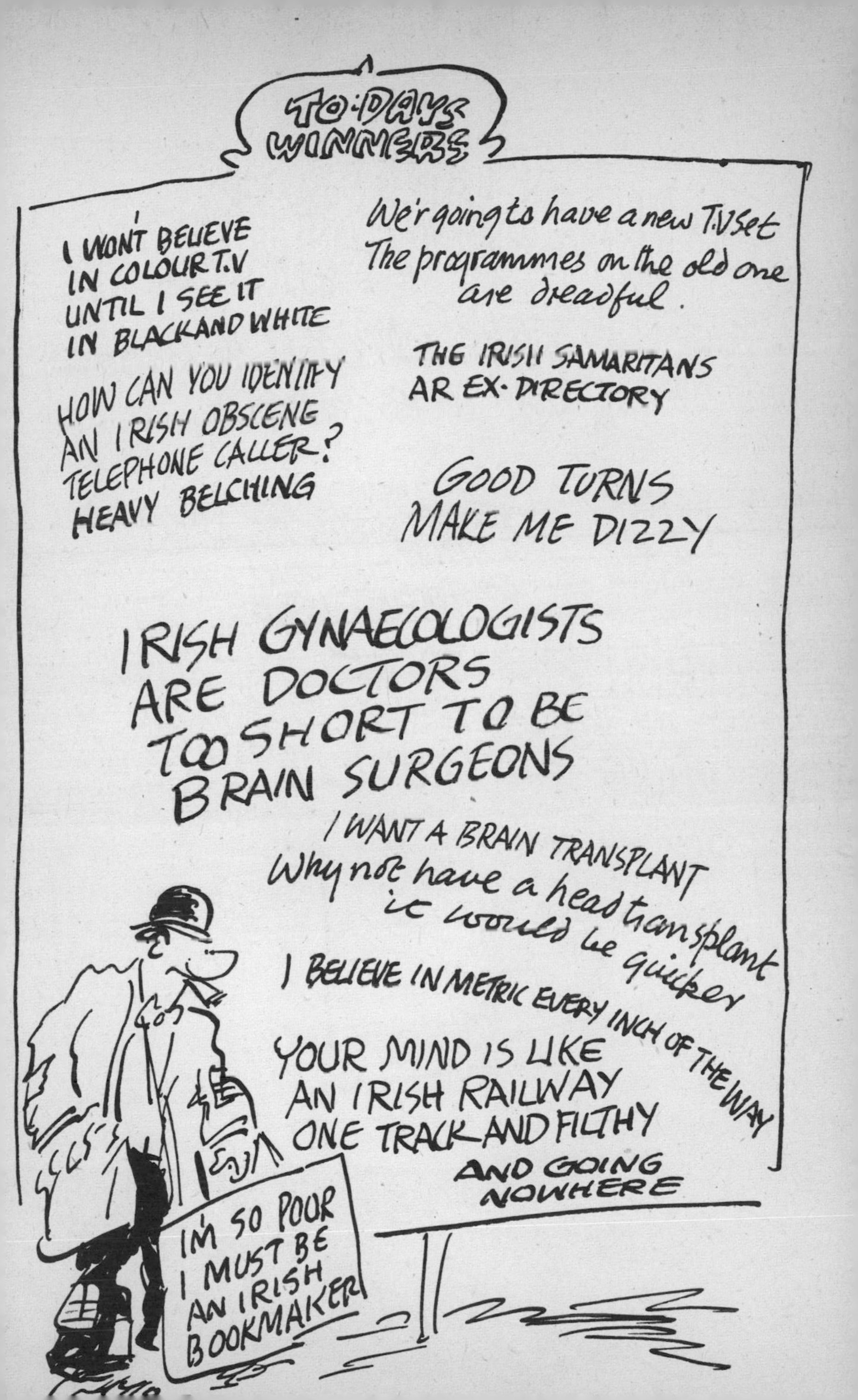

TO-DAYS WINNERS
I WONT BELIEVE IN COLOUR T.V UNTIL I SEE IT IN BLACK AND WHITE
We'r going to have a new T.V set The programmes on the old one are dreadful.
HOW CAN YOU IDENIIFY AN IRISH OBSCENE TELEPHONE CALLER? HEAVY BELCHING
THE IRISH SAMARITANS AR EX-DIRECTORY
GOOD TURNS MAKE ME DIZZY
IRISH GYNAECOLOGISTS ARE DOCTORS TOO SHORT TO BE BRAIN SURGEONS
I WANT A BRAIN TRANSPLANT
Why not have a head transplant it would be quicker
I BELIEVE IN METRIC EVERY INCH OF THE WAY
YOUR MIND IS LIKE AN IRISH RAILWAY ONE TRACK AND FILTHY
AND GOING NOWHERE
I'M SO POOR I MUST BE AN IRISH BOOKMAKER

A BIRD IN THE HAND IS A BLOODY NUISANCE WHEN YOU WANT TO PICK YOUR NOSE
I'd like opera if it wasn't far the singing.
IS FARTING CONTAGIOUS?
IRISH TRAFFIC WARDENS HAVE YELLOW BANDS ROUND THEIR HATS SO THAT YOU DON'T PARK ON THEIR HEADS
IRISH MILK BOTTLES ARE MADE OF MAGNIFYING GLASS TO MAKE THE MILK LOOK BIGGER
IRISH POLO MINTS HAVE THE HOLE ON THE OUTSIDE

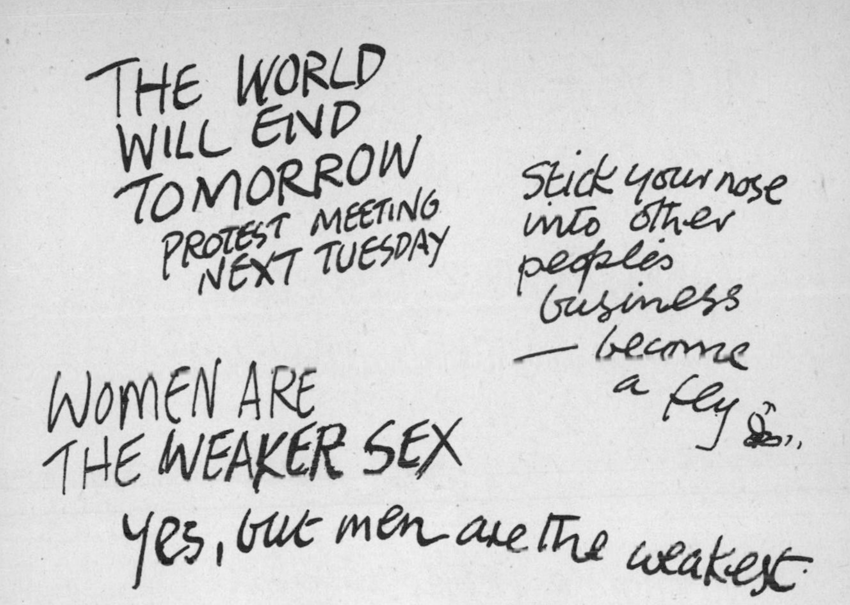
THE WORLD
WILL END
TOMORROW
PROTEST MEETING
NEXT TUESDAY
Stick your nose
into other
peoples
business
— become
a fly
WOMEN ARE
THE WEAKER SEX
yes, but men are the weakest

BE PESSIMISTIC -
PUT BRAN
ON YOUR PRUNES
BEWARE
RAMP

TAKE YOUR HOLIDAY IN WINTER
DECKCHAIRS ARE CHEAPER
Where do the Irish go
when they want to go
abroad ?
IRELAND
A LOT OF PEOPLE LEAVE
IRELAND EVERY YEAR
WELL? WHO WOULD WANT
TO STAY THERE?
BALLYMURPHY
WELCOMES
NEAT WRITERS
KILKENNY
CATS EYES
FOR 2
MILES

I don't think
Crazy paving
is all its
cracked up
to be.

VAL
DOONICAN
IS OFF
HIS
ROCKER

TOMORROW
IS JUST
ANOTHER
DAY

THE UPPER CRUST
ARE JUST A LOT OF CRUMBS
STICKING TOGETHER

Life is like a ten
speed cycle – there
are always some
gears you never use

IS THERE INTELLIGENT LIFE
IN IRELAND?
Yes, but I'm only here
for a fortnight

COW DUNG IS GOOD
600,000,000,000,000,000 FLIES
CAN'T BE WRONG

DRIVE LIKE
HELL, AND
YOU GET THERE

IT IS A GOOD THING
ELVIS IS DEAD
– HE'D BE PRETTY
LONELY ALL ALONE
IN HIS COFFIN IF HE
WERE STILL ALIVE

I WENT TO IRELAND BUT
IT WAS CLOSED.

Nobody is bald – some men just
have wider partings than others

THE ORIGINAL
POLO MINT
HOLE

NO
BILL
STICKERS

whats he done wrong?
NOTHING – ONLY DIED.

A ROLLING STONE GATHERS
NO NUTS IN MAY

97
THE BRAVEST SHOW ON EARTH
SKY-DIVING TEAM
PARACHUTES
PACKED
IN
IRELAND
AT LEAST LIFE IS ONLY TEMPORARY
YOU TOO CAN HAVE A BODY LIKE MINE
JUST LAY DOWN UNDER A TRACTOR
IRISH DRIVERS GIVE TWO-FINGER HAND SIGNALS ONLY
THE MAN IN THE MOON IS NEVER AS INTERESTING AS THE GIRL IN THE SUN
BE KIND TO YOUR FRIENDS. IF IT WASN'T FOR THEM YOU'D BE A TOTAL STRANGER
THIS WAY TO KISS THE GRAFFITI STONE

IRISH PEOPLE
When I get drunk on St Pattricks night Brummagem b'longs to me
WHAT DO YOU CALL A GOOD LOOKING IRISHMAN? — LUCKY

READ EVENING MAIL!
MISS IRELAND'S VITAL STATISTICS ARE 44-30-44
AND THE OTHER ARMS THE SAME
SUPPORT PSYCHOPATHS OR I'LL KILL YOU
I WAS GOING TO KILL MYSELF BY TAKING A BOTTLE FULL OF ASPRINS - BUT AFTER TAKING THE FIRST TWO I FELT MUCH BETTER.
80% OF IRISHMEN WEAR WELLIES — THE OTHER 28% CAN TIE SHOE-LACES
THE IRISH ARE BASTARDS
YES, THEY HAVE ENGLISH FATHERS.
IRISH HELLS ANGELS HAVE TRAINING WHEELS ON THEIR MOTORBIKES
I MAY NOT BE KNOWN OUTSIDE IRELAND, BUT IN WATERFORD I'M WORLD FAMOUS
I WASHED THE WRONG SIDE OF MY HANKY
BIRMINGHAM UNDER-PASS ON LOAN

I'M NO IDIOT YOU KNOW!
WHAT'S YOUR OPINION AGAINST A THOUSAND OTHERS
PADDY GOT A SPLINTER IN HIS FINGER - HE SCRATCHED HIS HEAD
IRISH MASOCHISTS TAKE PAIN KILLERS
I'M GOING TO TAKE UP MEDITATION - BETTER THAN SITTING AROUND ALL DAY DOING NOTHING
CLEAN EIRE ACTS LTD

LORD LUCAN WASN'T HERE
NEPOTISM RUNS IN THE FAMILY
BECOME A HERMIT KEEP GOAL FOR BELFAST UNITED
THIS SPACE FOR SALE
DON'T HAVE ANYTHING TO DO WITH POLITICS — VOTE HAUGHEY
IRISH STEIN IS THE NAME OF THE LAW
POLICE
POLICE
POLICE
POLIC
POLIC.
POLIC.
POLIC.

NEIGHBOURS ARE PEOPLE who Listen to your conversations through a WALL
YOUTH IS WASTED ON CHILDREN
THERE ARE THREE TYPES OF IRISHMAN— right-handed, left-handed and under-handed
THE TROUBLE WITH MOST PEOPLE IS THEIR TROUBLE
I MAY BE DAFT BUT I'M NOT BLOODY STUPID.
CHILDREN ARE SO EXPENSIVE ONLY THE POOR CAN AFFORD THEM
SIR FRANCIS DRAKE CIRCUMCISED THE GLOBE WITH A FORTY FOOT CUTTER

HE WHO LAUGHS LAST IS AN IRISHMAN WHO'S JUST UNDERSTOOD THE JOKE
PADDY WAS ENGAGED TO A CONTORTIONIST BUT SHE BROKE IT OFF
A GIRL SHOULD HANG ON TO HER YOUTH
BUT NOT WHILE HE'S DRIVING
SPOILSPORTS
BUILDING CLEANING LTD

IRISH QUEENS
PANSIES BAR
TOPLESS CHUCKER-OUTS
KING KONG WAS AN IRISH QUEEN

IS BEING GAY HEREDITARY?
No but Sterility is
IRISH THESPIANS AREN'T STRAIGHT ACTORS
GAY GHOSTS GIVE EACH OTHER THE WILLIES.
WILLIAM FITZPATRICK LOVES PATRICK FITZWILLIAM
IRISH POOFS!
YOU DON'T GET MANY HOMOS IN DUBLIN
I GET AS MANY AS I WANT DUCKY
KILROY WAS QUEER
BENDERS ENCYCLOPAEDIA
FROM OSCAR TO WYLDE
GAYS ARE A PAIN IN THE ARSE
There's no future in being gay
IF IT WASN'T FOR WOMEN WE'D ALL BE GAY.

WHY ARE SO MANY IRISHMEN GAY?
Have you seen the women?
YES! BUT HAVE YOU SEEN THE MEN?
Why *are* so many Irishmen gay?

When you're in a tight straight, you're in

QUEER STREET

IS AN ARSONIST A PRACTICING MEMBER OF GAY LIB?

HIS
HIS

I went to a gay 90's party. All the men were gay and the women were 90

GO GAY AND SAVE ON DUREX

GOD SAVE THE QUEENS

I WANTED SCENTED VASELINE

FOR SORES?

NO FOR CHAPS

I dont feel myself today

GOOD IT WAS A TERRIBLE HABIT ANYWAY

I DON'T CARE WHAT THE WORLD THINKS ABOUT ME
— I JUST HOPE MY MOTHER NEVER FINDS OUT
GEORGIE PORGIE PUDDING AND PIE
KISSED THE GIRLS AND MADE THEM CRY
WHEN THE BOYS CAME OUT TO PLAY
HE KISSED THEM TOO
HE'S FUNNY THAT WAY
I LIKE TREEFELLERS
WHY CAN'T YOU BE CONTENT WITH ONE LIKE EVERYBODY ELSE?
JEWELLERS
BLARNEY STONES
BEND DOWN AND LOOK IF YOU CAN SEE MY EAR-RING LOST DOWN THIS DRAIN
— I DARE YOU!

IRISH
RELIGION

WINSOR
AND
NEWTON
MAGIC
CROZIERS

EASTER IS CANCELLED THIS YEAR
THEY FOUND THE BODY

TERRY WOGAN FOR POPE

Keep the pope off the moon
It's the only bloody place he hasn't been

GOD LOVES YOU
So does Father O'Reilly.

THANK GOD I'M AN ATHEIST

Blessed Mary, we believe
That without sin thou didst conceive
Holy Virgin, this believing
May we sin without conceiving.

VATICAN APPROVED BIRTH CONTROL PILLS
TAKE ONE A NIGHT AND GET A HEADACHE

GOD IS NOT DEAD
HE JUST OVERSLEPT

CONTINUED NEXT COLUMN

GOD IS NOT DEAD.– IT WAS JUST A RUMOUR PUT ROUND BY PEOPLE WHO WANTED TO BECOME PRIESTS AND ONLY WORK ON SUNDAYS

Oh rosary, I love you ♫

I'VE NEVER BEEN SUPERSTITIOUS – TOUCH WOOD!

IRISH GIRLS GO OUT ON SATURDAY NIGHTS TO SOW WILD OATS, AND THEN GO TO CHURCH ON SUNDAY TO PRAY FOR CROP FAILURE

I've just been made a priest – can I go out and celibate?

LOVE THY NEIGHBOUR BUT DON'T GET CAUGHT

THERE WAS A YOUNG LADY CALLED ALICE
WHO PEED IN A VATICAN CHALICE
IT WASN'T THE COLD
THAT MADE HER SO BOLD
BUT SHEER BLOODY PROTESTANT MALICE

MONKS DO IT HABITUALLY

GOD IS NOT DEAD – JUST VERY SICK

HEAVEN IS MURPHY'S IDEA OF HELL

JESUS LOVES
THE IRISH PEOPLE
WHICH MEANS HE'S GOT
A GREAT SENSE OF HUMOUR
RELIGION IS DEAD IN IRELAND
SO THATS WHAT THE SMELL IS
SECOND HAND BIBLES
MAKE CHRISTMAS AN ANNUAL EVENT
HARDLY THUMPED

IRISH SEX
STRIP
this week.
OLD MOTHER RILEY
200 PETICOATS
EVERY PERFORMANCE.

WHAT WOULD YOU SAY TO A LITTLE NOOKIE?

'HELLO LITTLE NOOKIE'

Why is semen white and urine yellow?
So that you can tell whether you're coming or going.

IRISH BROTHELS HAVE BUNK BEDS

THERE ARE NO PROSTITUTES IN IRELAND!
NO IRISH GIRLS CAN'T EVEN GIVE IT AWAY

BE BI-SEXUAL AND
DOUBLE YOUR CHANCES

You're never alone
if you're a sex maniac.

MISS HUGHES
ROUGH SAILORS WELCOME
Rm 9

I THOUGHT ORAL CONTRACEPTION
WHAS WHEN YOU TALKED
YOUR WAY OUT OF IT

BURN YOUR BRAS
AND JOIN THE NATURAL FRONT

What is Irish Sex?
The number
between
five and seven

IRISHMEN ARE DREADFUL LOVERS
THEY WAIT FOR THE SWELLING TO GO DOWN

I want a contradictive pill
YOU'RE IGNORANT!
Yes, I know — six months

ARE VASECTOMIES HEREDITARY?

MURPHY HAD
A LITTLE LAMB
HIS CASE COMES UP
NEXT WEEK

DRAG ARTISTES
WANTED
MAIL
APPLY POST OFFICE

IRISH KISSES
ARE ALL BLARNEY

FRENCH KISS A PRINCE
AND HE TURNS INTO
A FROG

THE FRENCH ARE FROGS
THE IRISH ARE TOADS
— IN THE WHOLE!

THE FRENCH CALL IT SOIXANTE-NEUF
THE IRISH CALL IT 96

MAKE TEA - NOT LOVE
She was only the morse code operator's daughter
But she didit, didit, didit, diddiddidit
90% OF ACCIDENTS ARE CAUSED BY PEOPLE
90% OF PEOPLE ARE CAUSED BY ACCIDENTS
i'd rather be watching TV.
I DIDN'T KNOW YOU LIKE TRANSVESTITES, DEARIE
PADDY'S
SEX BOUTIQUE
IS A PROSTITUTE A RECEIVER OF SWOLLEN GOODS
VIBRATOR
£29.90

I LIKE MAKING LOVE TO IRISHMEN
THEY'RE BIG AND THICK!

Sex is a pain in the arse
YOU'RE OBVIOUSLY DOING IT WRONG

MAKE LOVE THE IRISH WAY
BACK TO BACK

CUNNILINGUS IS NOT AN IRISH AIRLINE
NO, IT'S A TONGUE-TWISTER

I've lost my virginity.
HAVE YOU STILL GOT THE RECEIPT

I can't stand sex.
TRY IT LYING DOWN

BE A FEMALE CHAUVENIST SOW
- MAKE HIM SLEEP IN THE WET PATCH

SEX IS EVIL, SO GO TO HELL

IRISHMEN ARE LIVING PROOF
THAT CAVEMEN SCREWED SHEEP.

What is incest?
IT'S A GAME FOR ALL THE FAMILY
No, it's rolling your own
COURSE NOT, IT'S THE THEORY OF RELATIVITY.
SAVE ENERGY · MAKE LOVE SLOWLY.
I'M INTO FLAGELATION, BESTIALITY, AND NECROPHILA
- AM I FLOGGING A DEAD HORSE?
CURE VIRGINITY
I thought a prick was something
you got from a need-le until
I discovered
SMIRNOFF
BRISTOL CREAM

LOVE COMES IN LITTLE SPURTS OR SQUIRTS

KOOKABURRA KOOKABURRA
SITS IN THE OLD GUM TREE
SCREWING EVERYTHING HE CAN SEE
STOP KOOKABURRA
STOP KOOKABURRA
THAT ONE HAS V.D.

IRISH
NYMPHOMANIACS
HATE
MEN

IRISH
Y-FRONTS
FIT
LIKE
A
GLOVE.

ANTIQUE
RUDE
SHOW
ADMISSION 30p

IRISH TOILETS
THE LAVATORY IS BOG
ATTENDANT IRISH
THE FUTURE OF IRELAND IS IN YOUR HANDS
THE MIGHTY QUINN WAS HERE

DON'T ALL SNIFF AT ONCE
IT WON'T GO ROUND

LARGE POLO MINTS
ARE NOT TO BE
EATEN

-TOILETS ARE WORTH EVERY PENNY
SPENT ON THEM

VENEREAL DISEASE
FOR VENEREALS ONLY

MAUREEN O'CONNELL
IF YOU'RE READING THIS
WE'RE THROUGH

YOU ARE ADVISED
TO WASH YOUR HANDS
AFTER USING
THIS TOWEL

THE PAINTER'S WORK
WAS ALL IN VAIN
THE SH*T HOUSE POET
STRIKES AGAIN

CONTRACEPTIVES HALF-PRICE FOR O.A.P.s
BULLDOG CLIPS
This is the worst chewing gum I ever tasted
BEWARE OF REMOULDS
SUBJECT TO VAT IF USED ON THE PREMISES
BUY TWO AND BE ONE JUMP AHEAD
Easy Rider
DANGER NO GRIP WHEN WET.
IN CASE OF FAILURE MARRY
IF THEY ARE TOO LONG CUT THE END OFF
The secrets in the little perforations
I PUT ONE OF THESE ON THE WRONG WAY ROUND AND WENT
My Dad says they don't work
LUCKY DIP.

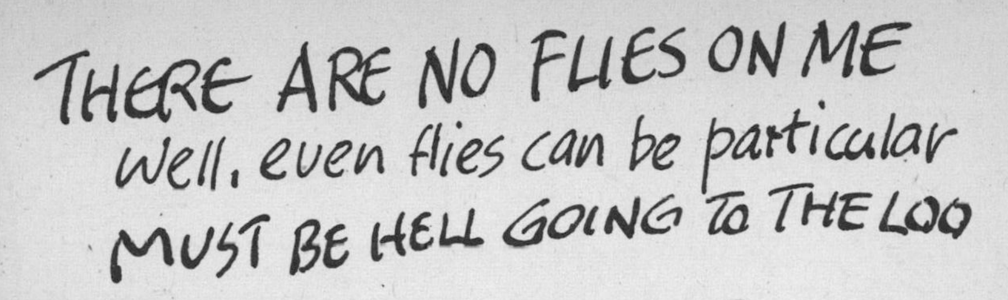
THERE ARE NO FLIES ON ME
Well, even flies can be particular
MUST BE HELL GOING TO THE LOO
DON'T SMOKE IN OUR TOILETS
AND WE WONT PEE IN YOUR ASHTRAYS

O TINKLE IS THE IRISH V.I.P.
SONG FOR EUROPE
PARADE OF BOATS 2-30

CRAP LINGUS
IF YOU WANT A WET SURPRISE PULL THE CHAIN BEFORE YOU RISE
DON'T SIT IN MEDITATION HURRY AND EVACUATE
NOTES
PLEASE PULL CHAIN SOME IRISHMEN EAT ANYTHING
TOILET OUT OF ORDER USE FLOOR BELOW
PROPERTY OF DAN DAN THE LAVATORY MAN

she was only the pilots daughter but she knew how to keep her cockpit clean
PULL THIS CHAIN THE ENGLISH NEED THE WATER
GOVERNMENT YOUTH TRAINING SCHEME
OFFICIAL INSTRUCTOR: T. KELLY

Here I sat
But not for long
The smell you left
was far too strong

BEWARE
OF
IRISH
LIMBO DANCERS

POLITICAL PROPAGANDA
FREE GOVERNMENT
POLICY PLEDGES

POWER TO THE
PEEPHOLE

The job isn't
finished until
the paperwork
is done

SMILE YOU'RE
ON GAME
FOR
A
LAUGH

IT'S NO USE SITTING
ON THE SEAT
THE CRABS IN HERE
CAN JUMP
SIX FEET

What is long and hard
and full of seamen
— a submarine
WHO NEED SEX EDUCATION
WHEN WE HAVE
TOILET WALLS.
CASTRATION
IS A LOAD
OF BALLS
IN DUBLIN'S FAIR CITY
WHERE THEY ALL WRITE GRAFFITI
HOT-AIR
HOT
DONNY
PRESS BUTTON
FOR 20 SECOND SPEECH
FROM IAN PAISLEY
WAS THE VERY FIRST
EUNUCH
TAKEN UNAWARES
IS THIS
THE SOURCE
OF THE
LIFFEY?